Be the Most Interesting Woman in the Room

This is a first publication 2024

Copyright © 2024 Bianchina Publishing House

All right reserved. No part of this publication may be reproduced or copied.

ISBN: 9798326274144

Chapter 1:   PG 07

Introduction

Embracing Your Unique Qualities and Strengths

The Art of Making a Lasting Impression

Chapter 2:   PG 12

Cultivating Confidence and Charisma

Building Self-Confidence Through Self-Awareness

Projecting Charisma and Presence in Social Settings

Chapter 3:   PG 19

Mastering the Art of Storytelling

Crafting Compelling Narratives to Engage and Entertain

Using Personal Anecdotes to Connect with Others

Chapter 4: PG 26

Developing Active Listening Skills

The Power of Paying Attention and Showing Genuine Interest

Asking Thoughtful Questions to Deepen Conversations

Chapter 5: PG 34

Navigating Networking Events with Ease

Strategies for Breaking the Ice and Approaching New People

Making Meaningful Connections in Professional Settings

Chapter 6: PG 42

The Importance of Body Language

Using Nonverbal Cues to Convey Confidence and Openness

Projecting Approachability and Warmth Through Body Language

Chapter 7:   PG 50

Elevating Your Elevator Pitch

Crafting a Succinct and Memorable Introduction

Tailoring Your Pitch to Different Audiences and Situations

Chapter 8:   PG 57

Standing Out in a Crowd

Finding Your Unique Voice and Perspective

Embracing Your Passions and Sharing Them Authentically

Chapter 9:   PG 66

Building Your Personal Brand

Identifying Your Strengths and Areas of Expertise

Communicating Your Value Proposition with Clarity and Conviction

Chapter 10:   PG 75

Getting Noticed in the Workplace

Strategies for Gaining Visibility and Recognition

Advocating for Yourself and Your Achievements

Chapter 11:   PG 83

Creating Memorable Interactions

Leaving a Positive Impression on Others Through Genuine Connection

Following Up and Maintaining Relationships After Initial Encounters

Chapter 12:   PG 91

Overcoming Social Anxiety and Nervousness

Techniques for Managing Nerves and Anxiety in Social Situations

Building Resilience and Confidence Over Time

Chapter 13:   PG 98

Conclusion

Embracing Your Uniqueness and Individuality

Committing to Being the Most Interesting Woman in Every Room

Disclaimer: The information provided in this Book is for educational and informational purposes only and is not intended as a substitute for professional advice or guidance. Readers are encouraged to seek support from qualified professionals as needed.

Chapter 1: Introduction

Embracing Your Unique Qualities and Strengths

In a world where conformity often seems like the norm, there's an undeniable allure to those who dare to be different, who embrace their unique qualities and strengths with unapologetic confidence. Imagine entering a room and instantly capturing the attention of everyone present, not because you're trying to impress, but simply because your authenticity radiates like a beacon amidst a sea of sameness. This is the power of embracing your individuality and harnessing your strengths to become the most captivating person in any setting.

At the heart of this concept lies the profound truth that each of us is inherently unique, possessing a blend of experiences, talents, quirks, and perspectives that no one else can replicate. Yet, in a society that often prioritizes conformity and fitting in, many of us find ourselves suppressing our true selves in favour of blending into the crowd. We dim our light to avoid standing out, fearing rejection or judgment from others. But what if we flipped the script and embraced what sets us apart instead?

Embracing your unique qualities and strengths isn't just about standing out for the sake of attention; it's about honouring your true self and allowing your authenticity to shine through in everything you do. It's about recognizing that your differences are not flaws to be hidden but rather assets to be celebrated. Whether you're an introvert with a passion for deep conversation, an artist with a unique vision, or a natural-born leader with the ability to inspire others, your distinctiveness is what makes you fascinating.

Becoming the most interesting person in the room isn't about conforming to some arbitrary standard of coolness or popularity; it's about embracing the full spectrum of who you are and leveraging your strengths to make meaningful connections with those around you. It's about being curious, open-minded, and unafraid to share your perspective, knowing that your authenticity will resonate with others on a deeper level than any superficial facade ever could.

When you embrace your uniqueness, you not only empower yourself to live a more fulfilling life, but you also inspire those around you to do the same. Your willingness to be authentic gives others permission to do the same, creating a ripple effect of self-acceptance and genuine connection. And in a world that often feels increasingly disconnected, there's nothing more compelling than someone who isn't afraid to be themselves.

So, embrace your quirks, flaunt your strengths, and own your story with pride. Because when you do, you'll not only become the most interesting person in the room—you'll also become a beacon of authenticity in a world that desperately needs it.

The Art of Making a Lasting Impression

Crafting a lasting impression isn't just about leaving a mark; it's about creating a legacy that resonates long after you've left the room. It's about mastering the subtle nuances of human interaction, understanding the power of perception, and harnessing the art of influence to captivate hearts and minds. To become the most interesting person in the room isn't merely a feat of charisma or charm; it's a mastery of the art of making a lasting impression.

Picture this: You walk into a room, and the energy shifts as all eyes turn to you, drawn by an invisible force that emanates from your very being. It's not just your appearance or demeanour that commands attention, but something deeper—an aura of authenticity, confidence, and charisma that leaves an indelible mark on everyone you encounter.

At the core of making a lasting impression lies the ability to connect with others on a profound level, to transcend the superficialities of small talk and delve into the realms of meaningful conversation. It's about listening as intently as you speak, making others feel truly seen and heard, and leaving them feeling uplifted and inspired by your presence.

But the art of making a lasting impression goes beyond mere words; it's about embodying your values and beliefs in everything you do. It's about living with purpose and passion, pursuing your dreams with unwavering determination, and inspiring others to do the same through your actions.

To become the most interesting person in the room is to embrace your uniqueness fully, to celebrate your strengths and quirks unabashedly, and to share your story with authenticity and vulnerability. It's about being unapologetically yourself in a room that often pressures us to conform to societal norms and expectations.

But perhaps most importantly, the art of making a lasting impression is rooted in kindness and empathy, in lifting others up and helping them shine as brightly as you do. It's about leaving a positive impact on the lives of those you encounter, no matter how fleeting the interaction may be.

So, as you embark on your journey to become the most interesting person in the room, remember this: It's not about impressing others or seeking validation; it's about living a life that inspires others to do the same. It's about leaving a legacy of love, kindness, and authenticity that transcends time and space, ensuring that your influence will be felt long after you're gone.

Chapter 2: Cultivating Confidence and Charisma

Building Self-Confidence Through Self-Awareness

Building self-confidence through self-awareness is like constructing a sturdy house on a solid foundation. Self-awareness serves as the cornerstone upon which true confidence is built, providing the clarity and understanding necessary to navigate life's challenges with poise and assurance. Let's delve into the intricate process of cultivating self-confidence through self-awareness in detail.

Understanding Self-Awareness: Self-awareness is the ability to recognize and understand your thoughts, emotions, and behaviours, as well as their impact on yourself and others. It involves introspection, observation, and a willingness to explore the depths of your inner world with honesty and curiosity. Developing self-awareness is not always easy; it requires courage to confront aspects of yourself that may be uncomfortable or challenging to acknowledge.

Benefits of Self-Awareness:

Clarity: Self-awareness provides clarity about your strengths, weaknesses, values, and goals. This clarity enables you to make informed decisions aligned with your authentic self, fostering a sense of purpose and direction.

Emotional Intelligence: Understanding your emotions allows you to manage them effectively, leading to greater emotional resilience and healthier relationships. Self-aware individuals are better equipped to express their feelings constructively and empathize with others.

Authenticity: Self-awareness empowers you to embrace your true self, free from the constraints of societal expectations or external validation. Authenticity breeds confidence, as you no longer feel the need to conform to others' standards but instead celebrate your uniqueness.

Self-Regulation: By recognizing your triggers and patterns of behaviour, you gain greater control over your actions and reactions. Self-regulation fosters a sense of inner calm and stability, reducing stress and anxiety in challenging situations.

Cultivating Self-Confidence Through Self-Awareness:

Identify Your Strengths and Weaknesses: Self-awareness involves recognizing both your areas of expertise and areas for growth. Celebrate your strengths and accomplishments, while also acknowledging areas where you can improve. Set realistic goals to develop skills and talents, boosting your confidence as you make progress.

Challenge Limiting Beliefs: Pay attention to your inner dialogue and identify any negative or self-limiting beliefs that undermine your confidence. Challenge these beliefs by questioning their validity and reframing them in a more empowering light. Replace self-criticism with self-compassion and encouragement.

Embrace Feedback: Solicit feedback from trusted friends, mentors, or colleagues to gain valuable insights into your blind spots and areas for development. Approach feedback with an open mind, viewing it as an opportunity for growth rather than as criticism. Use constructive feedback to refine your skills and enhance your performance.

Practice Mindfulness: Cultivate mindfulness through practices such as meditation, journaling, or mindful breathing. These practices help you develop greater self-awareness by grounding you in the present moment and fostering a non-judgmental awareness of your thoughts and emotions. Mindfulness enhances clarity of mind, emotional resilience, and overall well-being.

Celebrate Progress: Acknowledge and celebrate your achievements, no matter how small. Keep a gratitude journal to reflect on moments of success and personal growth. Celebrating your progress reinforces positive self-esteem and reinforces the belief in your abilities.

In Conclusion: Self-awareness is the cornerstone of self-confidence, providing the foundation upon which true empowerment is built. By cultivating self-awareness, you gain clarity, authenticity, and emotional resilience, enabling you to navigate life's challenges with confidence and grace. Embrace the journey of self-discovery with curiosity and compassion, knowing that true confidence arises from a deep understanding and acceptance of yourself.

Projecting Charisma and Presence in Social Settings

Projecting charisma and presence in social settings is akin to mastering the art of captivating an audience with your magnetism and charm. It's about exuding confidence, authenticity, and positive energy that draws people towards you effortlessly. Let's explore in detail the key elements and strategies for projecting charisma and presence in social settings:

1. Confidence: Confidence forms the cornerstone of charisma and presence. It's the belief in yourself and your abilities that radiates outward, making others feel comfortable and inspired in your presence. Cultivate confidence by setting realistic goals, celebrating your achievements, and embracing self-compassion. Practice confident body language, such as standing tall, maintaining eye contact, and speaking clearly and assertively.

2. Authenticity: Authenticity is the secret sauce of charisma—it's the genuine expression of your true self without pretence or façade. Embrace your quirks, vulnerabilities, and unique qualities, as they are what make you truly captivating. Be honest and transparent in your interactions, sharing your thoughts and feelings openly. Authenticity fosters trust and connection, as people are naturally drawn to those who are real and genuine.

3. Positive Energy: Charismatic individuals exude positive energy that uplifts and energizes those around them. Cultivate a positive mindset by focusing on gratitude, optimism, and kindness. Smile genuinely, laugh freely, and radiate warmth and enthusiasm in your interactions. Be mindful of your energy levels

and take steps to recharge when needed, whether through meditation, exercise, or spending time with loved ones.

4. Active Listening: Presence in social settings involves being fully engaged and attentive to the people around you. Practice active listening by giving others your undivided attention, maintaining eye contact, and nodding or paraphrasing to show understanding. Avoid interrupting or monopolizing the conversation, and instead, ask open-ended questions to encourage others to share their thoughts and experiences. By listening empathetically, you demonstrate respect and empathy, fostering deeper connections with others.

5. Body Language: Your body language speaks volumes about your presence and charisma. Project confidence and openness through your posture, gestures, and facial expressions. Maintain an open and relaxed stance, with arms uncrossed and shoulders relaxed. Use gestures to emphasize your points and express enthusiasm. Pay attention to your facial expressions, aiming for a genuine smile and warm eye contact to convey sincerity and approachability.

6. Storytelling: Charismatic individuals are skilled storytellers who captivate their audience with compelling narratives and anecdotes. Share personal stories and experiences that resonate

with others, weaving in elements of humour, vulnerability, and emotion. Use vivid language and imagery to paint a picture and evoke emotions in your listeners. Storytelling fosters connection and engagement, allowing others to see themselves reflected in your experiences.

7. Empathy and Understanding: Charisma isn't just about shining the spotlight on yourself—it's about making others feel seen, heard, and valued. Practice empathy by putting yourself in others' shoes and seeking to understand their perspectives and feelings. Show genuine interest in others' stories and experiences, and offer support and validation when needed. By demonstrating empathy and understanding, you create a safe and inclusive environment where people feel accepted and appreciated.

In conclusion, projecting charisma and presence in social settings is a blend of confidence, authenticity, positive energy, active listening, engaging body language, storytelling, and empathy. By cultivating these qualities and honing your social skills, you can become a magnetic presence that leaves a lasting impression on everyone you meet.

Chapter 3: Mastering the Art of Storytelling

Crafting Compelling Narratives to Engage and Entertain

Crafting compelling narratives is an art form that elevates conversation from mundane exchanges to captivating experiences. As the most interesting person in the room, your ability to engage and entertain through storytelling is a superpower that sets you apart. Let's dive into the intricate process of crafting compelling narratives in detail:

1. Know Your Audience: Understanding your audience is paramount to crafting narratives that resonate and captivate. Consider their interests, preferences, and cultural backgrounds to tailor your stories accordingly. Are they drawn to humour, adventure, or heartfelt moments? Adapt your storytelling style to cater to their tastes and make a genuine connection.

2. Start with a Strong Hook: The beginning of your narrative sets the tone and captures your audience's attention. Start with a compelling hook—a captivating anecdote, intriguing question, or surprising statement that piques curiosity and entices listeners to lean in and engage. The hook should be intriguing enough to

spark interest and set the stage for the rest of the story.

3. Build Tension and Conflict: Great narratives are driven by tension and conflict that keep listeners on the edge of their seats, eager to know what happens next. Introduce obstacles, challenges, or dilemmas that your protagonist faces, creating suspense and intrigue. As you navigate the rising action, escalate the stakes and build anticipation for the resolution.

4. Show, Don't Just Tell: Immerse your audience in the story by vividly painting scenes with descriptive language and sensory details. Allow them to experience the sights, sounds, smells, and emotions of the narrative firsthand, transporting them to the world you've created. Engage all their senses to evoke a visceral response and make the story come alive.

5. Incorporate Elements of Surprise and Revelation: Keep your audience engaged by introducing unexpected twists, turns, or revelations that defy their expectations. Surprise them with plot twists, unexpected outcomes, or hidden layers of meaning that add depth and complexity to the narrative. A well-timed revelation can leave a lasting impression and spark lively discussion.

6. Infuse Emotion and Vulnerability: Connect with your audience on a deeper level by infusing your narrative with authentic emotion and vulnerability. Share personal experiences, insights, and struggles that resonate with universal themes of love, loss, resilience, and growth. By baring your soul and showing your humanity, you invite empathy and forge genuine connections with your listeners.

7. Conclude with Impact: End your narrative with a satisfying conclusion that leaves a lasting impact on your audience. Wrap up loose ends, resolve conflicts, and leave listeners with a sense of closure or reflection. Consider incorporating a memorable takeaway or moral that resonates with the overarching theme of the story, leaving your audience with something to ponder long after the tale has ended.

8. Practice and Refine Your Craft: Crafting compelling narratives is a skill that improves with practice and feedback. Hone your storytelling abilities by regularly sharing stories with friends, family, or colleagues and soliciting their input. Pay attention to pacing, tone, and delivery, and be open to constructive criticism that helps you refine your craft and become an even more captivating storyteller.

In conclusion, crafting compelling narratives to engage and entertain is a multifaceted endeavour that requires empathy, creativity, and skilful execution. By knowing your audience, starting with a strong hook, building tension and conflict, showing rather than telling, incorporating surprises and revelations, infusing emotion and vulnerability, concluding with impact, and practicing your craft, you can become the most interesting person in the room whose stories leave a lasting impression on everyone fortunate enough to hear them.

Using Personal Anecdotes to Connect with Others

Using personal anecdotes to connect with others is a powerful way to build rapport, foster empathy, and create meaningful connections. Sharing your own experiences allows you to establish common ground, demonstrate vulnerability, and convey authenticity, making you more relatable and approachable. Let's explore how to effectively use personal anecdotes to connect with others in detail:

1. Choose Relevant Anecdotes: Select anecdotes that are relevant to the context of the conversation or the interests of the people you're engaging with. Consider the mood, tone, and topic of discussion, and choose stories that

resonate with the theme or help illustrate a point. Tailoring your anecdotes to the situation ensures they are more engaging and relatable to your audience.

2. Be Genuine and Authentic: Authenticity is key when sharing personal anecdotes. Be honest and transparent about your experiences, feelings, and reactions. Avoid embellishing or exaggerating details to make the story more dramatic; instead, focus on conveying the genuine emotions and insights that accompanied the experience. Authenticity fosters trust and strengthens connections with others.

3. Create Emotional Resonance: Infuse your anecdotes with emotion to evoke empathy and resonate with your audience on a deeper level. Share not only the events of the story but also the thoughts, feelings, and lessons learned along the way. By tapping into universal emotions such as joy, sadness, fear, or hope, you create a shared emotional experience that binds you to your listeners.

4. Show Vulnerability: Vulnerability is a powerful tool for building connection and intimacy with others. Don't be afraid to share stories that reveal your imperfections, insecurities, or failures. Showing vulnerability signals to others that you trust them enough to let your guard down and invites them to do the

same. It fosters empathy and understanding, strengthening the bond between you and your audience.

5. Use Vivid Descriptions and Details: Paint a vivid picture with your words by incorporating descriptive language and sensory details into your anecdotes. Help your audience visualize the scene, hear the sounds, and feel the emotions of the story as if they were experiencing it themselves. Engaging multiple senses enhances the impact of the narrative and makes it more memorable.

6. Invite Engagement and Interaction: Encourage engagement and interaction by inviting your audience to share their own experiences or thoughts related to the anecdote. Ask open-ended questions that encourage reflection or discussion, such as "Has anyone else ever been in a similar situation?" or "What would you have done in that scenario?" Creating a dialogue fosters deeper connections and mutual understanding.

7. Know Your Audience's Comfort Level: Be mindful of your audience's comfort level and boundaries when sharing personal anecdotes. Respect their privacy and sensitivities, and avoid sharing stories that may be too intimate or inappropriate for the setting. Pay attention to nonverbal cues and adjust your approach

accordingly to ensure everyone feels included and respected.

8. Practice Active Listening: Finally, practice active listening when sharing personal anecdotes. Pay attention to your audience's reactions and cues, such as nods, smiles, or expressions of empathy. Be present in the moment and respond empathetically to their responses, validating their feelings and experiences. Active listening fosters deeper connection and reciprocity in the conversation.

In conclusion, using personal anecdotes to connect with others is a powerful way to build rapport, foster empathy, and create meaningful connections. By choosing relevant anecdotes, being genuine and authentic, creating emotional resonance, showing vulnerability, using vivid descriptions and details, inviting engagement and interaction, knowing your audience's comfort level, and practicing active listening, you can effectively connect with others and forge lasting bonds based on shared experiences and understanding.

Chapter 4: Developing Active Listening Skills

The Power of Paying Attention and Showing Genuine Interest

The power of paying attention and showing genuine interest lies at the heart of meaningful human connections. In a world often characterized by distraction and disengagement, the simple act of giving someone your full attention and demonstrating authentic interest can have profound effects on relationships and interactions. Let's explore in detail the significance and impact of paying attention and showing genuine interest:

1. Validation and Respect: When you pay attention to someone and show genuine interest in what they have to say, you validate their experiences, thoughts, and feelings. This validation communicates that you respect them as an individual with unique perspectives and contributions. Feeling heard and understood fosters a sense of belonging and significance, strengthening the bond between you and the other person.

2. Building Trust and Rapport: Paying attention and showing genuine interest are key

components of building trust and rapport in relationships. By actively listening and engaging with others, you demonstrate that you care about their well-being and are invested in their success and happiness. Trust is built on the foundation of mutual respect, understanding, and support, all of which are nurtured through attentive and genuine interactions.

3. Deepening Understanding and Connection: Paying attention allows you to truly understand others' perspectives, experiences, and motivations. When you listen attentively and ask thoughtful questions, you gain insights into their thoughts, feelings, and values, deepening your connection with them. Genuine interest fosters empathy and compassion, enabling you to relate to others on a deeper level and forge meaningful connections based on shared understanding and mutual respect.

4. Fostering Empathy and Compassion: Showing genuine interest requires empathy—a willingness to step into someone else's shoes and see the world from their perspective. When you genuinely care about others' experiences and feelings, you cultivate compassion and empathy, which are essential components of healthy relationships and social connections. Empathy strengthens bonds by creating a sense of

understanding and solidarity, even in times of disagreement or conflict.

5. Enhancing Communication and Collaboration: Effective communication relies on active listening and genuine interest in the other person's point of view. When you pay attention and show genuine interest, you create an environment conducive to open and honest dialogue. This fosters collaboration, creativity, and problem-solving, as people feel empowered to share their ideas and work together towards common goals. Genuine interest cultivates a culture of inclusivity and respect, where everyone's contributions are valued and acknowledged.

6. Improving Personal and Professional Relationships: Paying attention and showing genuine interest are essential skills for building and maintaining positive personal and professional relationships. Whether with friends, family, colleagues, or clients, demonstrating attentiveness and sincere curiosity strengthens bonds and fosters mutual trust and respect. In professional settings, genuine interest can lead to better client relationships, increased employee engagement, and improved teamwork and collaboration.

7. Making a Positive Impact: Ultimately, paying attention and showing genuine interest have the

power to make a positive impact on people's lives. Whether through a kind word, a listening ear, or a genuine smile, your attentiveness and authentic interest can brighten someone's day, boost their confidence, or provide much-needed support during challenging times. Small gestures of genuine interest can have ripple effects, spreading kindness and positivity throughout your community and beyond.

In conclusion, paying attention and showing genuine interest are essential ingredients for building meaningful relationships, fostering trust and understanding, and making a positive impact on others' lives. By practicing active listening, empathy, and authentic engagement, you can cultivate deeper connections, enhance communication and collaboration, and create a more compassionate and inclusive world.

Asking Thoughtful Questions to Deepen Conversations

Asking thoughtful questions is a powerful way to deepen conversations, foster connection, and cultivate meaningful relationships. Thoughtful questions demonstrate genuine interest in the other person's thoughts, feelings, and experiences, inviting them to share more openly and authentically. Let's explore in detail the significance and impact of asking thoughtful questions:

1. Demonstrating Genuine Interest: When you ask thoughtful questions, you signal to the other person that you are genuinely interested in getting to know them better. Thoughtful questions go beyond surface-level inquiries and show that you care about their perspectives, opinions, and life experiences. This genuine interest lays the foundation for building rapport and strengthening connections.

2. Fostering Engagement and Active Listening: Asking thoughtful questions encourages active listening—the practice of fully concentrating on what the other person is saying without distractions. When you listen attentively to their responses, you demonstrate respect and validation for their thoughts and feelings. This creates a positive feedback loop where the other person feels heard and valued, leading to deeper engagement in the conversation.

3. Encouraging Reflection and Self-Discovery: Thoughtful questions prompt individuals to reflect on their beliefs, values, and experiences, leading to self-discovery and personal growth. By posing questions that encourage introspection and self-exploration, you create opportunities for deeper insight and

understanding. Thoughtful questions can also challenge assumptions and broaden perspectives, fostering intellectual curiosity and critical thinking.

4. Building Trust and Connection: Asking thoughtful questions builds trust by creating a safe and supportive space for open and honest communication. When people feel comfortable sharing their thoughts and feelings without fear of judgment, it strengthens the bond between them. Thoughtful questions demonstrate empathy and compassion, fostering a sense of connection and mutual understanding.

5. Enhancing Communication Skills: Practicing the art of asking thoughtful questions enhances your communication skills, including active listening, empathy, and emotional intelligence. Thoughtful questions require careful consideration of the other person's perspective and thoughtful responses that validate their experiences. As you hone these skills, you become a more effective communicator who can navigate conversations with grace and sensitivity.

6. Deepening Relationships: Thoughtful questions play a crucial role in deepening relationships over time. By consistently asking meaningful questions and actively listening to the answers, you create a foundation of trust,

respect, and mutual understanding. Deepening conversations lead to stronger connections and more fulfilling relationships, as both parties feel seen, heard, and valued for who they are.

7. Sparking Creativity and Innovation: Thoughtful questions can spark creativity and innovation by challenging conventional thinking and encouraging outside-the-box ideas. By asking questions that inspire curiosity and exploration, you invite new perspectives and fresh insights into the conversation. This creative exchange of ideas can lead to innovative solutions, breakthroughs, and opportunities for growth.

8. Strengthening Problem-Solving and Decision-Making: In professional settings, asking thoughtful questions is essential for problem-solving and decision-making. Thoughtful questions help clarify goals, identify obstacles, and explore potential solutions from different angles. By engaging in thoughtful dialogue and collaborative problem-solving, teams can make more informed decisions and achieve better outcomes.

In conclusion, asking thoughtful questions is a powerful tool for deepening conversations, fostering connection, and building meaningful relationships. By demonstrating genuine interest, encouraging reflection and self-discovery, building trust and connection, enhancing communication skills, deepening relationships, sparking creativity and innovation, and strengthening problem-solving and decision-making, thoughtful questions can enrich our interactions and lead to greater understanding and connection with others.

Chapter 5: Navigating Networking Events with Ease

Navigating networking events with ease requires a combination of confidence, social skills, and strategic approaches to breaking the ice and approaching new people. These events present valuable opportunities to expand your professional network, build relationships, and discover potential opportunities. Let's explore strategies for navigating networking events with ease, focusing on breaking the ice and approaching new people in detail:

1. Set Clear Goals: Before attending a networking event, clarify your objectives and goals. Determine what you hope to achieve, whether it's making new connections, seeking career opportunities, or gaining industry insights. Having clear goals will guide your interactions and help you make the most of the event.

2. Arrive Early: Arriving early to a networking event can alleviate some of the pressure and give you a chance to acclimate to the environment before it gets crowded. Use this time to familiarize yourself with the venue, scope out key attendees, and approach smaller groups or individuals with ease.

3. Use Open Body Language: Approachability is key when breaking the ice with new people. Use open body language, such as smiling, making eye contact, and uncrossing your arms, to signal approachability and receptiveness. A warm and welcoming demeanor will make others feel more comfortable engaging with you.

4. Start with a Simple Introduction: When approaching new people, start with a simple introduction that includes your name, profession, and a brief statement about why you're attending the event. Keep it concise and focused to make a positive first impression and initiate the conversation on a friendly note.

5. Ask Open-Ended Questions: Engage others in conversation by asking open-ended questions that invite them to share more about themselves. Avoid yes-or-no questions and instead ask about their professional background, interests, or recent projects. This demonstrates genuine interest and encourages deeper dialogue.

6. Listen Actively: Active listening is a crucial skill for building rapport and understanding others' perspectives. Pay close attention to what the other person is saying, nodding and paraphrasing to show understanding and interest. Listening attentively fosters a sense of connection and mutual respect.

7. Find Common Ground: Look for common interests, experiences, or connections that you share with the person you're speaking to. Finding common ground can create rapport and make the conversation more engaging. Whether it's a shared industry, hobby, or mutual acquaintance, highlighting commonalities can facilitate a meaningful connection.

8. Offer Value: Be proactive in offering value to the people you meet at networking events. Share insights, resources, or introductions that may be helpful to them based on their interests or needs. Providing value demonstrates your willingness to contribute and builds goodwill in your professional network.

9. Exit Gracefully: Know when to gracefully exit a conversation to mingle with other attendees. Politely thank the person for the conversation, exchange contact information if appropriate, and express your interest in staying connected. Exiting gracefully allows you to network with a wider range of people while maintaining positive interactions.

10. Follow Up After the Event: After the networking event, follow up with the people you met to reinforce the connection and continue the conversation. Send a personalized email or LinkedIn message referencing your discussion and expressing your interest in staying in touch.

Following up demonstrates your professionalism and commitment to nurturing relationships.

In conclusion, navigating networking events with ease requires strategic approaches to breaking the ice and approaching new people. By setting clear goals, arriving early, using open body language, starting with a simple introduction, asking open-ended questions, listening actively, finding common ground, offering value, exiting gracefully, and following up after the event, you can maximize your networking opportunities and build valuable professional relationships.

Making Meaningful Connections in Professional Settings

Making meaningful connections in professional settings is essential for building a strong network, advancing your career, and fostering personal growth. Meaningful connections go beyond surface-level interactions and involve establishing genuine relationships based on trust, mutual respect, and shared values. Let's explore strategies for making meaningful connections in professional settings in detail:

1. **Be Authentic:** Authenticity is the foundation of meaningful connections. Be genuine and true to yourself in your interactions with others. Share your values, interests, and experiences openly, and avoid putting on a facade or pretending to be someone you're not. Authenticity builds trust and allows others to connect with you on a deeper level.

2. **Listen Actively:** Effective communication is a two-way street that involves active listening as well as sharing your own thoughts and experiences. Practice active listening by giving your full attention to the person you're speaking with, asking clarifying questions, and reflecting on what they're saying. Listening attentively demonstrates respect and fosters deeper understanding and connection.

3. **Show Empathy and Understanding:** Empathy is the ability to understand and share the feelings of others. Show empathy by putting yourself in the shoes of the person you're connecting with and acknowledging their perspectives and emotions. Validate their experiences and demonstrate compassion and understanding. Empathy strengthens bonds and creates a sense of connection and camaraderie.

4. **Find Common Ground:** Look for common interests, experiences, or goals that you share with the person you're connecting with. Finding

common ground provides a basis for building rapport and fosters a sense of connection and camaraderie. Whether it's a shared industry, hobby, or mutual acquaintance, highlighting commonalities can facilitate meaningful conversations and connections.

5. Be Proactive and Approachable: Take initiative in reaching out to new people and initiating conversations. Be approachable and open to meeting new colleagues, clients, or industry peers. Attend networking events, conferences, and professional gatherings where you can connect with like-minded individuals. Proactively seeking out opportunities to connect demonstrates your enthusiasm and commitment to building relationships.

6. Offer Value and Support: Be generous in offering value and support to the people you meet in professional settings. Share insights, resources, or introductions that may be helpful to them based on their interests or needs. Provide support and encouragement when they face challenges or pursue opportunities. Offering value strengthens relationships and builds goodwill in your network.

7. Follow Up and Stay in Touch: After making an initial connection, follow up with the person to reinforce the relationship and continue the conversation. Send a personalized email or

LinkedIn message referencing your discussion and expressing your interest in staying in touch. Stay connected by regularly checking in, sharing updates, and offering support when needed. Consistent communication nurtures relationships and keeps them strong over time.

8. Be Respectful of Boundaries: Respect the boundaries and preferences of the people you're connecting with. Be mindful of their time, privacy, and communication preferences. Avoid being overly pushy or intrusive, and give them space if they're not ready to engage. Respecting boundaries demonstrates your professionalism and consideration for others' needs and preferences.

9. Foster a Culture of Collaboration: In professional settings, prioritize collaboration and teamwork as opportunities to make meaningful connections. Seek out opportunities to work with others on projects, initiatives, or volunteer activities. Collaboration fosters trust, respect, and camaraderie, leading to deeper connections and more fulfilling professional relationships.

10. Be Patient and Persistent: Building meaningful connections takes time and effort, so be patient and persistent in your networking efforts. Don't expect instant results or immediate gratification. Continue to nurture relationships over time, invest in building trust and rapport,

and be open to opportunities for growth and collaboration. Persistence pays off in the form of lasting, meaningful connections that enrich your professional and personal life.

In conclusion, making meaningful connections in professional settings requires authenticity, active listening, empathy, finding common ground, being proactive and approachable, offering value and support, following up and staying in touch, respecting boundaries, fostering a culture of collaboration, and being patient and persistent. By applying these strategies, you can build a strong network of meaningful professional relationships that contribute to your success and fulfilment in your career.

Chapter 6: The Importance of Body Language

Using Nonverbal Cues to Convey Confidence and Openness

Body language plays a crucial role in communication, influencing how others perceive us and interpret our messages. Nonverbal cues such as posture, gestures, facial expressions, and eye contact can convey a wealth of information about our thoughts, feelings, and intentions. In professional and social settings, mastering body language can help convey confidence, openness, and authenticity. Let's explore the importance of body language in detail and how to use nonverbal cues to convey confidence and openness:

1. Establishing Trust and Rapport: Body language is a powerful tool for building trust and rapport with others. When we display open and welcoming body language, such as smiling, making eye contact, and leaning slightly forward, we signal to others that we are approachable and trustworthy. These nonverbal cues create a positive first impression and lay the foundation for meaningful interactions.

2. Conveying Confidence and Authority: Confident body language exudes self-assurance and competence, influencing how others perceive our leadership abilities and expertise. Stand tall with shoulders back, maintain strong posture, and avoid slouching or fidgeting. Use expansive gestures and occupy space comfortably to convey confidence and authority. Confidence in your body language can enhance your credibility and command respect in professional and social settings.

3. Demonstrating Active Listening: Nonverbal cues such as nodding, maintaining eye contact, and facing the speaker indicate active listening and engagement. By mirroring the speaker's body language and providing attentive nonverbal feedback, you demonstrate that you are fully present and receptive to their message. Active listening fosters connection and understanding, strengthening relationships and communication.

4. Expressing Openness and Approachability: Open and welcoming body language invites others to approach us and engage in conversation. Uncross your arms, relax your shoulders, and maintain an open posture to signal receptivity and warmth. Smile genuinely and make eye contact to convey friendliness and approachability. These nonverbal cues create an

inviting atmosphere and encourage positive interactions.

5. Building Emotional Connection: Body language plays a crucial role in conveying emotions and building emotional connection with others. Genuine facial expressions, such as smiling or furrowing the brow, communicate our feelings and help others empathize with us. Use expressive gestures and body movements to convey enthusiasm, empathy, or concern, deepening emotional connection and understanding.

6. Enhancing Persuasion and Influence: Effective body language can enhance our ability to persuade and influence others. Adopting confident and persuasive gestures, such as nodding affirmatively or using open-handed gestures, can reinforce our verbal message and increase its impact. Maintain steady eye contact and use subtle mirroring techniques to establish rapport and build rapport with others, increasing receptivity to our ideas and proposals.

7. Adapting to Cultural Norms: It's important to be mindful of cultural differences in body language when communicating with individuals from diverse backgrounds. Gestures, posture, and facial expressions may carry different meanings in different cultures, so it's essential to adapt our body language to align with cultural

norms and avoid misunderstandings or unintentional offense.

8. Practicing Self-Awareness: Developing self-awareness is key to effectively using body language to convey confidence and openness. Pay attention to your own nonverbal cues and how they may be perceived by others. Notice any unconscious habits or gestures that may undermine your message, such as crossing your arms or avoiding eye contact, and work to adjust them to align with your desired communication goals.

In conclusion, body language is a powerful form of communication that can influence how others perceive us and interpret our messages. By mastering nonverbal cues and using them to convey confidence, openness, and authenticity, we can enhance our relationships, build trust and rapport, and become more effective communicators in both professional and social settings.

Projecting Approachability and Warmth Through Body Language

Projecting approachability and warmth through body language is essential for fostering positive connections and building rapport with others. When we convey openness and warmth through our nonverbal cues, we invite others to engage with us and create an atmosphere of trust and comfort. Let's explore in detail how to project approachability and warmth through body language:

1. Facial Expressions: Facial expressions are one of the most powerful indicators of approachability and warmth. A genuine smile is universally recognized as a sign of friendliness and openness. When greeting others or engaging in conversation, smile warmly and naturally to convey approachability and put others at ease. Avoid frowning or displaying tense expressions, as these can signal disinterest or hostility.

2. Eye Contact: Maintaining appropriate eye contact is crucial for projecting approachability and warmth. When speaking with someone, make direct eye contact to show attentiveness and interest in the conversation. Avoid staring intently, which can be perceived as aggressive or confrontational. Instead, maintain a comfortable level of eye contact while also allowing for natural breaks to prevent overwhelming the other person.

3. Open Posture: An open posture communicates approachability and receptivity to others. Keep your body language relaxed and open by

uncrossing your arms and legs. Stand or sit with your body facing towards the person you're interacting with, rather than turning away or crossing your limbs, which can create barriers and signal defensiveness.

4. Mirroring and Matching: Mirroring and matching the body language of others can help create a sense of connection and rapport. Subtly mimic the other person's gestures, posture, and facial expressions to establish rapport and convey warmth. However, be mindful of mirroring too closely or too obviously, as it can come across as insincere or manipulative. Instead, aim for natural and authentic mirroring that enhances rapport without drawing attention to itself.

5. Active Listening Cues: Active listening cues such as nodding, leaning forward slightly, and using affirmative verbal cues (e.g., "I see," "That's interesting") convey genuine interest and engagement in the conversation. Use these nonverbal cues to signal that you're fully present and attentive to the other person's words. Avoid appearing distracted or disengaged, as this can undermine your efforts to project approachability and warmth.

6. Gestures of Welcome: Incorporate gestures of welcome into your body language to signal openness and invitation. For example, extend

your hand for a handshake when greeting someone, or offer a friendly wave or nod of acknowledgment from a distance. These small gestures communicate warmth and hospitality, making others feel welcome and valued in your presence.

7. Tone of Voice: The tone of your voice can significantly impact how approachable and warm you come across in conversation. Speak in a calm, friendly tone, with a moderate volume and pace. Avoid speaking too loudly or too softly, as this can create barriers to communication. Aim for a warm and inviting tone that conveys genuine interest and warmth.

8. Personal Space: Respect personal space boundaries when interacting with others to avoid making them feel uncomfortable or intruded upon. Maintain an appropriate distance that allows for comfortable conversation without invading the other person's space. Be mindful of cultural differences in personal space preferences and adjust accordingly to ensure that you project approachability and warmth in a respectful manner.

In conclusion, projecting approachability and warmth through body language involves a combination of facial expressions, eye contact, posture, mirroring, active listening cues, gestures of welcome, tone of voice, and respect for personal space. By incorporating these nonverbal cues into your interactions, you can create a welcoming and inviting atmosphere that fosters positive connections and meaningful relationships with others.

Chapter 7: Elevating Your Elevator Pitch

Crafting a succinct and memorable introduction is essential for making a strong first impression and sparking interest in yourself or your endeavours. Whether you're introducing yourself at a networking event, a professional meeting, or a social gathering, a well-crafted introduction sets the tone for further interaction and leaves a lasting impression. Here's how to create a memorable introduction in detail:

1. Start with Your Name: Begin your introduction by stating your name clearly and confidently. Your name is the first thing people want to know when they meet you, so make sure to pronounce it clearly and enunciate each syllable if necessary. Using a firm handshake while stating your name can further reinforce your confidence and presence.

2. Provide Relevant Context: After stating your name, provide some brief context that gives others a sense of who you are and what you do. This could include your profession, area of expertise, or current role. Keep this part concise and focused, highlighting the most relevant information that you want others to remember about you.

3. Share Your Unique Selling Proposition (USP): Highlight what sets you apart from others by sharing your unique selling proposition (USP). This could be a specific skill, accomplishment, or characteristic that distinguishes you from the crowd. Focus on what makes you valuable or interesting to others and how you can contribute to their needs or interests.

4. Inject Personality and Passion: Add a personal touch to your introduction by injecting some personality and passion into your delivery. Share a brief anecdote, hobby, or interest that reflects your personality and values. This helps to humanize you and make you more relatable to others, creating a connection beyond your professional identity.

5. Tailor to Your Audience: Consider the context and audience when crafting your introduction and tailor it accordingly. If you're introducing yourself at a professional networking event, focus on your professional background and relevant accomplishments. In a social setting, you may want to highlight your personal interests and hobbies that resonate with the group.

6. Practice Conciseness and Clarity: Keep your introduction concise and to the point, avoiding unnecessary details or jargon that may confuse

or overwhelm your audience. Aim to deliver your introduction in 30 seconds to a minute, capturing attention without monopolizing the conversation. Practice your introduction beforehand to ensure clarity and confidence in your delivery.

7. End with a Call to Action or Question: Conclude your introduction with a call to action or question that prompts further engagement. This could be inviting others to connect with you, asking for their input or advice on a relevant topic, or proposing a follow-up meeting or conversation. Ending with a clear next step encourages interaction and keeps the conversation flowing.

8. Be Memorable: Finally, strive to make your introduction memorable by leaving a positive impression on your audience. Consider incorporating a memorable or unexpected element, such as a catchy phrase or interesting fact about yourself, that makes you stand out in their minds. Aim to leave your audience intrigued and eager to learn more about you.

In summary, crafting a succinct and memorable introduction involves stating your name clearly, providing relevant context about yourself, sharing your unique selling proposition, injecting personality and passion, tailoring to your audience, practicing conciseness and clarity, ending with a call to action or question, and striving to be memorable. By following these steps, you can create an introduction that captivates attention, sparks interest, and sets the stage for meaningful interactions and connections.

Tailoring Your Pitch to Different Audiences and Situations

Tailoring your pitch to different audiences and situations is essential for effectively communicating your message and achieving your objectives. Whether you're pitching a product, service, idea, or yourself, adapting your pitch to resonate with the specific needs, interests, and preferences of your audience can significantly increase your chances of success. Here's how to tailor your pitch to different audiences and situations in detail:

1. Understand Your Audience: Before crafting your pitch, take the time to understand your audience's demographics, preferences, and priorities. Consider factors such as their industry, job role, level of expertise, interests, and pain points. Conduct research or gather insights through conversations to gain a deeper

understanding of what matters most to your audience.

2. Identify Key Pain Points and Benefits: Tailor your pitch to address the specific pain points and challenges faced by your audience. Identify the problems or needs that your product, service, or idea can solve and emphasize the benefits and value proposition that are most relevant to your audience. Frame your pitch in terms of how it can help your audience overcome obstacles, achieve their goals, or improve their lives.

3. Customize Your Messaging: Adapt your messaging and language to resonate with the preferences and communication style of your audience. Use terminology and jargon that are familiar to them, demonstrating your understanding of their industry or field. Highlight specific features, benefits, or use cases that are most compelling to your audience and align with their interests and priorities.

4. Highlight Relevant Examples or Case Studies: Provide real-world examples, case studies, or testimonials that illustrate how your product, service, or idea has benefited similar clients or customers. Tailor your examples to reflect the specific challenges or objectives of your audience, showcasing relevant success stories that resonate with their needs and aspirations. Concrete evidence of your value proposition can

bolster credibility and build trust with your audience.

5. Customize Your Delivery Style: Consider the context and setting in which you'll be delivering your pitch and tailor your delivery style accordingly. Adjust your tone, pace, and demeanour to match the expectations and norms of your audience and situation. For example, a pitch delivered to a corporate boardroom may require a more formal and polished presentation style, while a pitch delivered at a startup event may benefit from a more casual and energetic approach.

6. Address Potential Objections: Anticipate potential objections or concerns that your audience may have and proactively address them in your pitch. Offer solutions or counterarguments that alleviate their concerns and demonstrate your readiness to address any challenges or reservations they may have. Showing empathy and understanding towards your audience's concerns can build credibility and instil confidence in your pitch.

7. Foster Engagement and Interaction: Encourage engagement and interaction during your pitch by inviting questions, soliciting feedback, or facilitating discussions with your audience. Tailor your approach to match the preferences and dynamics of your audience,

whether it's a formal Q&A session, interactive polling, or small group discussions. Engaging your audience in dialogue fosters a sense of ownership and investment in your pitch and increases the likelihood of a positive outcome.

8. Adapt in Real-Time: Be prepared to adapt your pitch in real-time based on the feedback, reactions, or questions you receive from your audience. Stay flexible and responsive to the dynamics of the situation, adjusting your messaging or presentation as needed to address emerging concerns or opportunities. Demonstrating agility and responsiveness reinforces your credibility and demonstrates your commitment to meeting the needs of your audience.

In summary, tailoring your pitch to different audiences and situations involves understanding your audience, identifying key pain points and benefits, customizing your messaging, highlighting relevant examples or case studies, adapting your delivery style, addressing potential objections, fostering engagement and interaction, and adapting in real-time. By taking a strategic and audience-centric approach to your pitch, you can maximize its impact and achieve your objectives effectively.

Chapter 8: Standing Out in a Crowd

Finding Your Unique Voice and Perspective

Standing out in a crowd requires finding and embracing your unique voice and perspective—the qualities that set you apart from others and make you memorable. In a world filled with noise and competition, authenticity and originality are key to making a lasting impression and attracting attention. Here's how to find your unique voice and perspective in detail:

1. Know Yourself: Start by gaining a deep understanding of yourself—your values, passions, strengths, and experiences. Reflect on what makes you unique and different from others. Consider your personal and professional journey, including your successes, challenges, and lessons learned. Self-awareness is the foundation upon which you can build your unique voice and perspective.

2. Identify Your Core Values and Beliefs: Clarify your core values and beliefs—the principles that guide your decisions and actions. Your values serve as the compass that directs your life and shapes your worldview. Aligning

your voice and perspective with your values enables you to communicate authentically and with conviction. Embrace your values as the cornerstone of your unique identity.

3. Embrace Your Passions and Interests: Explore your passions and interests, as they often reveal insights into your unique voice and perspective. What topics or activities ignite your curiosity and enthusiasm? What issues or causes do you feel strongly about? Embracing your passions allows you to speak with authenticity and authority, capturing the attention of others who share similar interests.

4. Cultivate Your Expertise: Invest time and effort in developing expertise in your chosen field or area of interest. Whether it's through formal education, hands-on experience, or continuous learning, deepen your knowledge and skills to establish credibility and authority. Becoming an expert in your niche positions you as a thought leader and allows you to offer valuable insights from your unique perspective.

5. Embrace Your Uniqueness: Celebrate your quirks, idiosyncrasies, and individuality—these are what make you stand out from the crowd. Don't be afraid to express your personality authentically, even if it means being different or unconventional. Embracing your uniqueness gives you a distinct voice and perspective that

resonates with others who appreciate authenticity and originality.

6. Find Your Narrative: Craft a compelling narrative that communicates your story, values, and vision. Your narrative is the thread that weaves together your experiences and beliefs into a cohesive and memorable story. Share your journey, including the challenges you've overcome and the lessons you've learned along the way. A compelling narrative draws people in and leaves a lasting impression.

7. Be Fearlessly Authentic: Authenticity is magnetic—it attracts others to you and fosters genuine connections. Don't be afraid to speak your truth and express your opinions, even if they differ from the mainstream. Authenticity requires vulnerability and courage, but it also earns respect and admiration from those who value honesty and sincerity.

8. Stay Curious and Open-Minded: Maintain a curious and open-minded attitude towards life and the world around you. Be receptive to new ideas, perspectives, and experiences, as they can broaden your horizons and enrich your unique voice. Seek out diverse sources of inspiration and engage with people who challenge and expand your thinking.

9. Continuously Refine and Evolve: Your unique voice and perspective are not static—they evolve and grow over time. Stay committed to continuous self-reflection and refinement, seeking opportunities to further develop and express your authentic self. Embrace feedback and constructive criticism as opportunities for growth and improvement.

10. Be Consistent and Authentic: Consistency is key to building a strong and recognizable personal brand. Stay true to your values, beliefs, and style across all your interactions and communications. Authenticity shines through when you're genuine and consistent in how you present yourself to the world.

In summary, finding your unique voice and perspective involves knowing yourself, identifying your core values and beliefs, embracing your passions and interests, cultivating expertise, embracing your uniqueness, crafting a compelling narrative, being fearlessly authentic, staying curious and open-minded, continuously refining and evolving, and being consistent and authentic. By embracing your authenticity and expressing your unique voice, you can stand out in a crowd and leave a lasting impression on others.

Embracing Your Passions and Sharing Them Authentically

Embracing your passions and sharing them authentically is a powerful way to connect with others, express yourself, and find fulfilment in life. Your passions are the things that ignite your enthusiasm, drive, and creativity—they are the fuel that propels you forward and gives meaning to your endeavours. When you authentically share your passions with others, you not only inspire and engage those around you but also create deeper connections based on shared interests and values. Here's how to embrace your passions and share them authentically in detail:

1. Identify Your Passions: Take the time to explore and identify the activities, interests, and pursuits that truly light you up and bring you joy. Reflect on what makes you feel alive and fulfilled—whether it's a hobby, a cause, a creative pursuit, or a professional endeavor. Your passions may evolve over time, so stay open to discovering new interests and passions along the way.

2. Understand Why Your Passions Matter: Reflect on why your passions are meaningful to you and how they align with your values, goals, and aspirations. Your passions often reflect your

deepest desires, values, and beliefs, providing a sense of purpose and direction in life. Understanding the significance of your passions empowers you to embrace them fully and share them authentically with others.

3. Integrate Your Passions into Your Life: Make time for your passions and prioritize activities that bring you joy and fulfilment. Integrate your passions into your daily routine and lifestyle, whether it's through dedicated hobby time, creative projects, or pursuing opportunities related to your passions in your professional or personal life. Cultivating a passion-driven lifestyle enriches your overall well-being and happiness.

4. Be Vulnerable and Authentic: Authenticity is key to effectively sharing your passions with others. Be willing to be vulnerable and share your genuine thoughts, feelings, and experiences related to your passions. Avoid putting on a facade or pretending to be someone you're not—people resonate most with authenticity and sincerity. By being true to yourself, you invite others to connect with you on a deeper level.

5. Share Your Stories and Experiences: Use storytelling as a powerful tool to convey your passions and experiences authentically. Share personal anecdotes, insights, and lessons learned from your journey with your passions. Your

stories humanize your experiences and make them relatable to others, creating a connection based on shared experiences and emotions.

6. Demonstrate Enthusiasm and Energy: Infuse your communication and interactions with enthusiasm and energy when discussing your passions. Let your genuine excitement and passion shine through in your voice, facial expressions, and body language. Passion is contagious, and your enthusiasm will naturally inspire and captivate those around you.

7. Seek Out Like-Minded Communities: Connect with others who share your passions by seeking out like-minded communities, groups, or events. Surrounding yourself with people who understand and appreciate your passions creates a supportive environment where you can freely express yourself and share your interests without judgment.

8. Be Open to Collaboration and Learning: Stay open to collaboration and learning opportunities that arise from sharing your passions with others. Embrace opportunities to collaborate with others who share similar interests or expertise, whether it's through joint projects, workshops, or mentorship. Keep an open mind and be receptive to new ideas and perspectives that can enrich your understanding and enjoyment of your passions.

9. Inspire and Empower Others: Use your passion and enthusiasm to inspire and empower others to pursue their own passions and dreams. Share your knowledge, skills, and resources generously with others who are interested in exploring similar interests or pursuits. Serve as a role model and mentor to those who are seeking guidance and encouragement along their own passion-driven journey.

10. Stay True to Yourself: Above all, stay true to yourself and your passions, even in the face of challenges or setbacks. Your passions are an integral part of who you are, and embracing them authentically is essential for your personal growth and fulfilment. Trust in yourself and your ability to navigate life with passion, purpose, and authenticity.

In summary, embracing your passions and sharing them authentically involves identifying your passions, understanding why they matter, integrating them into your life, being vulnerable and authentic, sharing your stories and experiences, demonstrating enthusiasm and energy, seeking out like-minded communities, being open to collaboration and learning, inspiring and empowering others, and staying true to yourself. By embracing your passions authentically, you not only enrich your own life but also inspire and connect with others in meaningful and profound ways.

Chapter 9: Building Your Personal Brand

Identifying Your Strengths and Areas of Expertise

Building your personal brand starts with identifying your strengths and areas of expertise— the unique qualities and skills that set you apart from others and define your professional identity. Your personal brand is how you present yourself to the world and how others perceive you, so understanding your strengths and expertise is essential for shaping your brand and positioning yourself for success. Here's how to identify your strengths and areas of expertise in detail:

1. Self-Reflection: Start by engaging in self-reflection to identify your strengths, skills, and areas of expertise. Consider your past experiences, achievements, and accomplishments—both personally and professionally. Reflect on the tasks or projects that come naturally to you and where you excel. Think about the feedback you've received from others and the qualities they appreciate about you.

2. Conduct a Skills Assessment: Conduct a comprehensive assessment of your skills and competencies to identify areas of expertise. This can include technical skills, soft skills, and specialized knowledge relevant to your field or industry. Assess your proficiency in each skill and prioritize those that you excel in or have a passion for developing further.

3. Seek Feedback from Others: Reach out to colleagues, mentors, friends, and family members for feedback on your strengths and areas of expertise. Ask them to identify your key strengths and qualities, as well as any areas where they see you excelling or making a significant impact. External perspectives can provide valuable insights and help you gain a more well-rounded understanding of your strengths.

4. Review Past Achievements: Review your past achievements and successes to identify patterns or themes that highlight your areas of expertise. Look for commonalities among your accomplishments and the skills or qualities that contributed to your success. Analyze the impact you've made in previous roles or projects and the specific strengths you leveraged to achieve results.

5. Assess Your Passion and Interest: Consider your passions and interests when identifying

your areas of expertise. What topics or activities do you feel most passionate about? Where do you invest your time and energy willingly? Your passion and interest in a particular subject or field often indicate areas where you have the potential to excel and develop expertise over time.

6. Utilize Assessments and Tools: Consider using self-assessment tools or personality assessments to gain further insights into your strengths and areas of expertise. Tools such as StrengthsFinder, Myers-Briggs Type Indicator (MBTI), or DISC assessment can provide valuable information about your personality traits, strengths, and preferred working styles.

7. Analyse Industry Trends and Market Demand: Stay informed about industry trends, market demand, and emerging opportunities within your field or industry. Identify areas where there is a high demand for specific skills or expertise and assess how your strengths align with these opportunities. Positioning yourself in high-demand areas can enhance your marketability and relevance.

8. Set Goals for Development: Based on your assessment of your strengths and areas of expertise, set goals for further development and growth. Identify areas where you'd like to enhance your skills or expand your expertise and

create a plan for achieving these goals. Invest in ongoing learning and professional development to continually strengthen your personal brand and stay competitive in your field.

9. Build Your Brand Narrative: Once you've identified your strengths and areas of expertise, craft a compelling brand narrative that communicates your unique value proposition to your target audience. Articulate your strengths, skills, and expertise in a clear and concise manner, highlighting how they differentiate you from others and contribute to your overall brand identity.

10. Seek Opportunities to Showcase Your Expertise: Look for opportunities to showcase your expertise and strengths through your work, projects, and interactions with others. Volunteer for challenging assignments, take on leadership roles, and actively participate in industry events, conferences, or speaking engagements. Position yourself as a thought leader and subject matter expert within your niche to elevate your personal brand and expand your influence.

In summary, identifying your strengths and areas of expertise is a foundational step in building your personal brand. Through self-reflection, skills assessment, feedback from others, review of past achievements, assessment of passion and interest, utilization of assessments and tools, analysis of industry trends, setting goals for development, crafting a brand narrative, and seeking opportunities to showcase your expertise, you can create a compelling personal brand that reflects your unique strengths, skills, and expertise.

Communicating Your Value Proposition with Clarity and Conviction

Communicating your value proposition with clarity and conviction is essential for capturing the attention of your audience and persuading them to engage with your products, services, or ideas. Your value proposition is the unique promise of value that you offer to your customers or stakeholders, highlighting the benefits and advantages of choosing your offering over alternatives. Here's how to communicate your value proposition effectively:

1. Start with a Clear Statement: Begin by crafting a concise and compelling statement that clearly articulates your value proposition. Keep it simple and straightforward, avoiding technical jargon or industry buzzwords that may confuse your audience. Your statement should answer the question: "What value do I provide and why should my audience care?"

2. Focus on Customer Benefits: Centre your value proposition around the benefits and outcomes that your audience will experience by engaging with your offering. Highlight how your product or service solves their problems, meets their needs, or fulfils their desires. Frame your message in terms of the value it delivers to the customer, rather than just listing features or capabilities.

3. Provide Evidence and Proof Points: Support your value proposition with evidence and proof points that validate your claims and build credibility. This could include customer testimonials, case studies, data points, or third-party endorsements that demonstrate the tangible results and benefits of your offering. Concrete evidence helps to reinforce your value proposition and alleviate any scepticism.

4. Differentiate Yourself from Competitors: Clearly communicate what sets you apart from competitors and why your offering is superior or unique. Identify your competitive advantages, whether it's innovative features, superior quality, competitive pricing, exceptional customer service, or a differentiated brand experience. Highlighting your points of differentiation helps to position you as the preferred choice in the eyes of your audience.

5. Use Engaging and Persuasive Language: Craft your message using language that is engaging, persuasive, and impactful. Use power words and emotional triggers to evoke a strong response from your audience. Appeal to their emotions, aspirations, and pain points to create a connection and resonate with their needs and desires. A compelling narrative can make your value proposition more memorable and compelling.

6. Tailor Your Message to Your Audience: Adapt your value proposition to resonate with different audience segments or target demographics. Customize your messaging based on factors such as demographics, psychographics, preferences, and buying behaviors. Tailoring your message to the specific needs and interests of your audience increases its relevance and effectiveness.

7. Be Authentic and Transparent: Communicate your value proposition with authenticity and transparency, demonstrating honesty and integrity in your messaging. Avoid exaggerations or false promises that may erode trust and credibility. Be upfront about what you can deliver and how you can help your audience, fostering a sense of trust and reliability.

8. Reiterate and Reinforce: Consistently reinforce your value proposition across all

touchpoints and channels where you interact with your audience. Repeat your key messages and value propositions consistently to reinforce their importance and memorability. Use multiple formats and mediums, such as website copy, social media posts, marketing collateral, and sales presentations, to amplify your message and reach your audience effectively.

9. Invite Action and Engagement: Encourage your audience to take action and engage with your offering by providing clear calls-to-action that prompt them to learn more, make a purchase, or contact you for further information. Create a sense of urgency or excitement around your value proposition to motivate immediate action and drive conversions.

10. Seek Feedback and Iterate: Regularly seek feedback from your audience to gauge the effectiveness of your value proposition and messaging. Listen to their input, analyse their responses, and make adjustments as needed to optimize your communication strategy. Continuously iterate and refine your value proposition based on real-world insights and feedback from your audience.

In summary, communicating your value proposition with clarity and conviction involves crafting a clear and compelling statement, focusing on customer benefits, providing evidence and proof points, differentiating yourself from competitors, using engaging language, tailoring your message to your audience, being authentic and transparent, reiterating and reinforcing your message, inviting action and engagement, and seeking feedback to continuously improve. By effectively communicating the value you offer, you can build trust, engage your audience, and drive success in your endeavours.

Chapter 10: Getting Noticed in the Workplace

Strategies for Gaining Visibility and Recognition

Getting noticed in the workplace requires more than just doing good work; it involves actively strategizing to gain visibility and recognition for your contributions. Whether you're aiming for a promotion, seeking opportunities for growth, or simply looking to make a positive impact, getting noticed can pave the way for advancement and career success. Here are some strategies for gaining visibility and recognition in the workplace in detail:

1. Excel in Your Role: First and foremost, consistently deliver high-quality work in your current role. Strive for excellence in everything you do, meeting or exceeding expectations and deadlines. Demonstrating competence and reliability forms the foundation for gaining visibility and recognition in the workplace.

2. Take Initiative: Don't wait for opportunities to come to you—actively seek them out. Take initiative by volunteering for challenging projects, proposing innovative ideas, or offering to take on additional responsibilities. Proactively

look for ways to add value to your team or organization, and don't be afraid to step outside your comfort zone.

3. Build Strong Relationships: Cultivate positive relationships with colleagues, managers, and other stakeholders in your organization. Invest time in networking and building connections across different departments and levels of the organization. Building rapport and trust with others can increase your visibility and open doors to new opportunities.

4. Communicate Effectively: Communicate your achievements, ideas, and contributions effectively to others. Articulate your accomplishments in a clear and concise manner, highlighting the impact they've had on the organization. Share your insights and perspectives in meetings, presentations, or written communications, demonstrating your expertise and thought leadership.

5. Seek Feedback and Recognition: Seek feedback from colleagues, mentors, and supervisors on your performance and contributions. Use feedback as an opportunity for growth and improvement, and incorporate constructive criticism into your professional development efforts. Additionally, don't hesitate to celebrate your successes and

accomplishments, both publicly and privately, to garner recognition for your hard work.

6. Demonstrate Leadership Qualities: Demonstrate leadership qualities, even if you're not in a formal leadership role. Take ownership of projects, inspire others with your vision and enthusiasm, and lead by example through your actions and behaviours. Showing initiative, resilience, and adaptability can position you as a leader within your team or organization.

7. Share Your Expertise: Share your knowledge, skills, and expertise with others in your organization. Offer to mentor junior colleagues, lead training sessions or workshops, or contribute to internal knowledge-sharing platforms. By sharing your expertise generously, you can establish yourself as a subject matter expert and gain visibility among your peers.

8. Leverage Social Capital: Take advantage of social capital by aligning yourself with influential individuals or groups within your organization. Build relationships with key stakeholders who can advocate for you and support your career advancement goals. Seek out mentors or sponsors who can provide guidance, advice, and opportunities for growth.

9. Be Proactive in Promoting Yourself: Don't be shy about promoting yourself and your

achievements in a professional and tactful manner. Update your LinkedIn profile with your accomplishments, skills, and expertise. Share updates and successes on social media or internal communication channels, positioning yourself as a valuable asset to your organization.

10. Stay Visible and Engaged: Stay visible and engaged in your workplace by participating in team meetings, events, and activities. Contribute actively to discussions and brainstorming sessions, and offer your input on important decisions or initiatives. By staying engaged and involved, you'll remain on the radar of decision-makers and influencers within your organization.

In summary, gaining visibility and recognition in the workplace requires a proactive approach that combines excellence in performance, initiative-taking, relationship-building, effective communication, leadership, knowledge-sharing, leveraging social capital, self-promotion, and active engagement. By implementing these strategies consistently, you can increase your visibility, enhance your reputation, and pave the way for career advancement and success in your organization.

Advocating for Yourself and Your Achievements

Advocating for yourself and your achievements is a crucial skill that can help you gain recognition, advance your career, and achieve your goals. It involves confidently and effectively communicating your value, accomplishments, and contributions to others, including colleagues, managers, and decision-makers. Here's how to advocate for yourself and your achievements:

1. Know Your Worth: Start by recognizing your own value and the contributions you bring to the table. Reflect on your skills, strengths, achievements, and the impact you've had in your role or organization. Understand the value you provide and believe in your ability to make a difference.

2. Keep Track of Your Achievements: Maintain a record of your accomplishments, projects, and successes over time. Document quantifiable results, awards, positive feedback from clients or colleagues, and any other evidence of your contributions. Having a clear record of your achievements will help you advocate for yourself more effectively.

3. Be Confident and Assertive: Approach self-advocacy with confidence and assertiveness. Stand tall, maintain eye contact, and speak

clearly when communicating your achievements and goals. Believe in yourself and your abilities, and convey that confidence to others through your demeanour and communication style.

4. Prepare Your Elevator Pitch: Craft a succinct and compelling elevator pitch that highlights your key achievements, skills, and value proposition. Practice delivering your pitch in a concise and impactful manner, ensuring that you can confidently communicate your value in various situations, from casual conversations to formal presentations.

5. Use Data and Evidence: Support your claims with data, evidence, and concrete examples of your achievements. Quantify the results of your work whenever possible, using metrics, numbers, or percentages to demonstrate the impact you've had on the organization. Hard data adds credibility to your assertions and strengthens your case for recognition.

6. Be Proactive in Seeking Opportunities: Don't wait for recognition to come to you—proactively seek out opportunities to showcase your achievements and contributions. Volunteer for high-profile projects, take on leadership roles, and actively participate in discussions and decision-making processes. Position yourself as a proactive and engaged team member who is committed to making a difference.

7. Advocate for Yourself in Performance Reviews: Use performance reviews as a platform to advocate for yourself and your achievements. Come prepared with a list of your accomplishments, goals achieved, and areas where you've exceeded expectations. Be proactive in discussing your career aspirations, development opportunities, and desired areas of growth with your manager.

8. Seek Feedback and Endorsements: Seek feedback from colleagues, mentors, and supervisors on your performance and contributions. Use positive feedback and endorsements from others to bolster your case for recognition and advancement. Request recommendations or testimonials from individuals who can attest to your skills, professionalism, and impact.

9. Be Persistent and Resilient: Advocating for yourself may require persistence and resilience, especially if you encounter resistance or pushback from others. Don't be discouraged by setbacks or rejections—continue to assert yourself confidently and pursue opportunities to showcase your value. Stay focused on your goals and maintain a positive attitude, even in the face of challenges.

10. Support Others and Build Allies: Support your colleagues and peers in their own efforts to

advocate for themselves. Build alliances and foster positive relationships with others who can support and champion your cause. By collaborating with and supporting others, you can strengthen your network and create mutual opportunities for recognition and advancement.

In summary, advocating for yourself and your achievements involves knowing your worth, keeping track of your accomplishments, being confident and assertive, preparing your elevator pitch, using data and evidence to support your claims, being proactive in seeking opportunities, advocating for yourself in performance reviews, seeking feedback and endorsements, being persistent and resilient, and supporting others while building allies. By mastering the art of self-advocacy, you can amplify your impact, gain recognition, and advance your career with confidence and success.

Chapter 11: Creating Memorable Interactions

Leaving a Positive Impression on Others Through Genuine Connection

Creating memorable interactions and leaving a positive impression on others through genuine connection involves fostering meaningful and authentic relationships that resonate with people on a deeper level. It's about being present, empathetic, and sincere in your interactions, making others feel valued and understood. Here are some strategies for creating memorable interactions and leaving a positive impression:

1. Be Present and Engaged: Give your full attention to the person you're interacting with and be fully present in the moment. Put away distractions such as your phone or other devices and focus on listening actively and empathetically. Show genuine interest in what the other person is saying and convey openness through your body language and facial expressions.

2. Practice Active Listening: Listen attentively to the other person's words, thoughts, and emotions without interrupting or rushing to respond. Practice active listening by

paraphrasing what they've said, asking clarifying questions, and validating their feelings. Demonstrate empathy and understanding by reflecting back their emotions and experiences.

3. Show Authenticity and Vulnerability: Be genuine and authentic in your interactions, allowing yourself to be vulnerable and transparent. Share your own thoughts, feelings, and experiences openly, fostering a sense of trust and connection with others. Authenticity breeds authenticity, and showing vulnerability can encourage others to do the same, deepening the connection.

4. Find Common Ground: Look for common interests, experiences, or values that you share with the other person and use them as a basis for connection. Finding common ground creates a sense of rapport and camaraderie, making the interaction more enjoyable and memorable for both parties.

5. Practice Empathy and Compassion: Put yourself in the other person's shoes and strive to understand their perspective and emotions. Show empathy and compassion by acknowledging their feelings, validating their experiences, and offering support or encouragement when needed. Empathetic connections leave a lasting impression and strengthen relationships.

6. Be Positive and Upbeat: Maintain a positive and upbeat attitude during interactions, radiating warmth and positivity. Smile genuinely, use humour when appropriate, and focus on highlighting the bright side of things. Positive energy is contagious and can uplift others, leaving them with a positive impression of you.

7. Be Memorable and Unique: Inject elements of creativity, spontaneity, or surprise into your interactions to make them memorable and distinctive. Share interesting stories, ask thought-provoking questions, or offer unexpected compliments or gestures of kindness. Leaving a memorable impression requires standing out in a positive and meaningful way.

8. Follow Up and Stay Connected: After the interaction, follow up with the person to express gratitude, continue the conversation, or offer ongoing support or assistance. Send a personalized email, text message, or handwritten note to show that you value the connection and are invested in maintaining it over time. Staying connected reinforces the positive impression and fosters long-term relationships.

9. Practice Gratitude and Appreciation: Express gratitude and appreciation for the other person's time, insights, and contributions during the interaction. Acknowledge their efforts and positive qualities, and express genuine thanks

for the impact they've had on you. Gratitude cultivates goodwill and strengthens bonds, leaving a positive and lasting impression.

10. Be Consistent in Your Interactions: Consistency is key to leaving a positive impression over time. Be consistent in your behavior, communication style, and values across different interactions, ensuring that others know what to expect from you. Consistency builds trust and reliability, solidifying your reputation as someone who leaves a positive impression wherever they go.

In summary, creating memorable interactions and leaving a positive impression on others through genuine connection involves being present and engaged, practicing active listening, showing authenticity and vulnerability, finding common ground, practicing empathy and compassion, being positive and upbeat, being memorable and unique, following up and staying connected, practicing gratitude and appreciation, and being consistent in your interactions. By prioritizing genuine connections and meaningful relationships, you can leave a positive and lasting impression on others in both personal and professional settings.

Following Up and Maintaining Relationships After Initial Encounters

Following up and maintaining relationships after initial encounters is essential for nurturing connections, building rapport, and fostering long-term relationships. It demonstrates your commitment to building meaningful connections and staying engaged with others over time. Here are some strategies for following up and maintaining relationships after initial encounters:

1. Send a Personalized Follow-Up Message: After your initial encounter, send a personalized follow-up message to express gratitude for the interaction and reiterate your interest in staying connected. Tailor your message to reference specific topics or points discussed during the encounter to show that you were attentive and engaged.

2. Reference Shared Interests or Goals: Reference any shared interests, goals, or experiences discussed during the initial encounter in your follow-up communication. This demonstrates that you were listening and that you value the connection enough to follow up on common ground.

3. Provide Value or Relevant Information: Offer to provide value or share relevant information

that may be of interest to the other person based on your conversation. This could include articles, resources, or introductions to individuals in your network who could benefit them. Providing value strengthens the relationship and demonstrates your willingness to contribute.

4. Schedule a Follow-Up Meeting or Call: Propose a specific date and time for a follow-up meeting or call to continue the conversation and deepen the connection. Having a concrete plan in place demonstrates your commitment to maintaining the relationship and allows you to stay top of mind.

5. Stay Active on Social Media: Stay connected with the other person on social media platforms such as LinkedIn, Twitter, or Facebook. Engage with their content by liking, commenting, or sharing posts relevant to your shared interests or goals. Social media provides an additional channel for maintaining visibility and staying connected.

6. Attend Networking Events or Industry Functions Together: Look for opportunities to attend networking events or industry functions together to further build your relationship in person. Meeting face-to-face reinforces the connection and allows for more meaningful interactions outside of formal settings.

7. Show Genuine Interest and Support: Demonstrate genuine interest in the other person's success, goals, and achievements. Offer support, encouragement, and congratulations on their milestones or accomplishments. Showing that you care about their well-being fosters trust and strengthens the relationship.

8. Be Responsive and Reliable: Be responsive and reliable in your communication and follow-up efforts. Respond promptly to emails, calls, or messages from the other person, and follow through on any commitments or promises you've made. Consistency and reliability build trust and credibility over time.

9. Keep the Conversation Going: Keep the conversation going by regularly checking in with the other person and finding opportunities to reconnect. Share updates on your own activities or projects, and ask about their recent experiences or achievements. Keeping the lines of communication open helps to maintain the relationship and keep it relevant.

10. Nurture the Relationship Over Time: Nurture the relationship over time by investing in ongoing interactions and meaningful connections. Stay connected through regular communication, periodic check-ins, and occasional meetings or outings. Building a strong foundation of trust and mutual respect

takes time and effort but is essential for sustaining long-term relationships.

In summary, following up and maintaining relationships after initial encounters involves sending personalized follow-up messages, referencing shared interests or goals, providing value or relevant information, scheduling follow-up meetings or calls, staying active on social media, attending networking events together, showing genuine interest and support, being responsive and reliable, keeping the conversation going, and nurturing the relationship over time. By implementing these strategies consistently, you can build and sustain meaningful connections that enrich your personal and professional life.

Chapter 12: Overcoming Social Anxiety and Nervousness

Techniques for Managing Nerves and Anxiety in Social Situations

Overcoming social anxiety and nervousness can be challenging, but with practice and patience, you can learn techniques to manage your feelings and navigate social situations more comfortably. Here are some techniques for managing nerves and anxiety in social situations:

1. Practice Relaxation Techniques: Practice relaxation techniques such as deep breathing, progressive muscle relaxation, or mindfulness meditation to calm your mind and body before entering social situations. These techniques can help reduce physical tension and promote a sense of calmness and relaxation.

2. Challenge Negative Thoughts: Challenge negative thoughts and beliefs that contribute to your social anxiety. Instead of assuming the worst-case scenario or anticipating rejection, try to adopt a more balanced and realistic perspective. Remind yourself that most people are not as critical or judgmental as you might fear.

3. Gradual Exposure: Gradually expose yourself to social situations that trigger anxiety, starting with less intimidating settings and gradually increasing the level of challenge over time. This exposure allows you to build confidence and resilience gradually, without overwhelming yourself.

4. Set Realistic Goals: Set realistic and achievable goals for yourself in social situations. Instead of aiming for perfection or trying to eliminate all anxiety, focus on small steps and accomplishments that move you closer to your goals. Celebrate your progress, no matter how small.

5. Focus on the Present Moment: Practice mindfulness techniques to stay focused on the present moment rather than dwelling on past experiences or worrying about the future. Pay attention to your surroundings, your breathing, and your physical sensations, grounding yourself in the here and now.

6. Use Positive Self-Talk: Use positive self-talk to challenge self-doubt and boost your confidence. Replace negative thoughts with affirmations and reminders of your strengths and abilities. Encourage yourself with phrases like "I can handle this" or "I am worthy of connection."

7. Prepare and Rehearse: Prepare for social situations by anticipating potential challenges and planning how you will respond. Rehearse conversations or presentations in advance to feel more confident and prepared. Having a plan can help reduce uncertainty and anxiety.

8. Focus on Others: Shift your focus away from yourself and onto others in social situations. Listen actively, ask questions, and show genuine interest in the people you're interacting with. By focusing on the needs and experiences of others, you can distract yourself from your own anxiety.

9. Use Visualization: Use visualization techniques to imagine yourself successfully navigating social situations with confidence and ease. Visualize yourself feeling calm, comfortable, and confident while interacting with others. Visualization can help reinforce positive beliefs and reduce anxiety.

10. Seek Support: Seek support from friends, family members, or a therapist who can provide encouragement, guidance, and perspective. Talking about your feelings with someone you trust can help you feel understood and supported, and a therapist can offer evidence-based strategies for managing social anxiety.

11. Take Small Steps: Start by taking small steps outside your comfort zone, gradually exposing

yourself to social situations that trigger anxiety. Celebrate each step forward, no matter how small, and be patient with yourself as you work toward overcoming social anxiety.

Remember that overcoming social anxiety is a gradual process, and it's okay to progress at your own pace. Be kind to yourself and acknowledge the courage it takes to face your fears and step outside your comfort zone. With time, practice, and persistence, you can learn to manage your nerves and anxiety in social situations more effectively.

Building Resilience and Confidence Over Time

Building resilience and confidence over time is a gradual process that involves self-awareness, self-care, and intentional practice. Here are some strategies to help you cultivate resilience and confidence:

1. Cultivate Self-Awareness: Start by developing a deeper understanding of yourself, including your strengths, weaknesses, values, and beliefs. Reflect on past experiences and identify how you've responded to challenges in the past. Recognizing your patterns of behaviour and thought can help you build resilience by

understanding how you typically cope with adversity.

2. Set Realistic Goals: Set achievable goals for yourself that align with your values and aspirations. Break larger goals into smaller, manageable steps, and celebrate your progress along the way. Achieving goals boosts confidence and provides a sense of accomplishment, reinforcing your belief in your abilities.

3. Embrace Challenges: View challenges as opportunities for growth and learning rather than obstacles to be avoided. Embracing challenges helps you build resilience by developing your problem-solving skills and adaptability. When faced with a difficult situation, remind yourself that you have the ability to overcome it and emerge stronger on the other side.

4. Practice Self-Compassion: Be kind and compassionate toward yourself, especially during times of difficulty or failure. Treat yourself with the same warmth and understanding that you would offer to a friend facing similar challenges. Practice self-compassion by acknowledging your efforts and progress, even if things don't go as planned.

5. Develop Coping Strategies: Identify healthy coping strategies that help you manage stress

and navigate difficult emotions. This could include exercise, mindfulness meditation, journaling, or seeking support from others. Having a toolkit of coping strategies can help you effectively manage adversity and build resilience over time.

6. Cultivate a Growth Mindset: Adopt a growth mindset, believing that your abilities and intelligence can be developed through effort and perseverance. Embrace failures and setbacks as opportunities for learning and growth rather than signs of inadequacy. Focus on continuous improvement and learning from your experiences.

7. Build a Support Network: Surround yourself with supportive friends, family members, mentors, and colleagues who uplift and encourage you. Seek out positive relationships and connections that provide emotional support, practical advice, and constructive feedback. Building a strong support network can bolster your resilience and confidence.

8. Celebrate Your Successes: Take time to acknowledge and celebrate your successes, no matter how small. Recognize your achievements and milestones along the way, and give yourself credit for your hard work and perseverance. Celebrating your successes boosts confidence and reinforces your belief in your abilities.

9. Learn from Setbacks: View setbacks as valuable learning experiences rather than reasons to give up or doubt yourself. When faced with a setback, take time to reflect on what you've learned and how you can grow from the experience. Use setbacks as opportunities to course-correct and move forward with renewed determination.

10. Practice Gratitude: Cultivate an attitude of gratitude by focusing on the positive aspects of your life and expressing appreciation for the people and things that bring you joy. Practicing gratitude can help shift your perspective, reduce stress, and increase resilience in the face of adversity.

Building resilience and confidence takes time and effort, but with consistent practice and self-care, you can develop the skills and mindset needed to thrive in the face of challenges. Remember to be patient with yourself and celebrate your progress along the way.

Chapter 13: Conclusion

Embracing Your Uniqueness and Individuality

Embracing your uniqueness and individuality is not just about accepting who you are, but celebrating it as your greatest strength. It's about recognizing that your differences are what make you truly remarkable and valuable. By embracing your quirks, passions, and perspectives, you invite others to do the same, fostering a culture of authenticity and inclusivity. Embracing your uniqueness allows you to stand out from the crowd, to bring your own flavour to every interaction and situation. It empowers you to navigate the world with confidence, knowing that your authentic self is your greatest asset. So, embrace your uniqueness, honour your individuality, and dare to shine brightly as the one-of-a-kind masterpiece that you are.

Committing to Being the Most Interesting Woman in Every Room

Committing to being the most interesting woman in every room is not about seeking attention or validation from others, but rather about embracing your own unique qualities and passions with confidence and authenticity. It's about stepping into your power and owning your presence, knowing that you have something valuable to offer in any social setting. Here's how you can commit to being the most interesting woman in every room in detail:

1. Cultivate Your Curiosity: Stay curious and open-minded about the world around you. Seek out new experiences, ideas, and perspectives that pique your interest. Whether it's exploring different cultures, trying new hobbies, or delving into unfamiliar subjects, embrace opportunities for growth and learning.

2. Develop a Range of Interests: Cultivate a diverse range of interests and hobbies that reflect your passions and personality. Whether you're passionate about art, science, literature, or adventure, let your curiosity guide you and pursue activities that ignite your enthusiasm. Having a variety of interests makes you more well-rounded and engaging in conversations.

3. Share Your Stories and Experiences: Don't be afraid to share your stories, experiences, and insights with others. Your unique perspective and life experiences can offer valuable insights

and spark meaningful conversations. Be authentic and vulnerable in sharing your journey, and be open to listening to others' stories as well.

4. Embrace Your Uniqueness: Celebrate what makes you unique and special. Whether it's your sense of humour, your creativity, or your unconventional interests, embrace your individuality with pride. Don't be afraid to let your personality shine and express yourself authentically in every situation.

5. Continuously Learn and Grow: Commit to lifelong learning and personal growth. Stay informed about current events, trends, and developments in areas that interest you. Challenge yourself to step outside your comfort zone and explore new opportunities for personal and professional development.

6. Cultivate Confidence and Presence: Cultivate confidence in yourself and your abilities. Stand tall, speak with conviction, and own your space in every room you enter. Projecting confidence and presence not only attracts attention but also commands respect and admiration from others.

7. Be a Good Listener: Being interesting isn't just about talking; it's also about listening attentively to others. Show genuine interest in what others have to say, ask thoughtful

questions, and engage in active listening. By being a good listener, you create space for meaningful connections and conversations to flourish.

8. Stay Authentic and Genuine: Above all, stay true to yourself and your values. Avoid trying to impress others or pretending to be someone you're not. Authenticity is magnetic and attractive, and being genuine in your interactions will draw people to you naturally.

9. Be Empathetic and Compassionate: Show empathy and compassion toward others. Be attentive to their needs, offer support and encouragement, and celebrate their successes. Building meaningful connections with others requires genuine care and empathy for their well-being.

10. Inspire Others: Lead by example and inspire others to embrace their own uniqueness and individuality. Share your passions, follow your dreams, and encourage others to do the same. By being confident and authentic in who you are, you empower others to do the same and create a ripple effect of inspiration and positivity.

Committing to being the most interesting woman in every room is not about seeking validation or approval from others, but about embracing your own unique qualities, passions, and experiences with confidence and authenticity. By cultivating curiosity, sharing your stories, embracing your uniqueness, continuously learning and growing, cultivating confidence and presence, being a good listener, staying authentic and genuine, showing empathy and compassion, and inspiring others, you can confidently assert your presence and make a lasting impression in any social setting.

www.ingramcontent.com/pod-product-compliance
Lightning Source LLC
Chambersburg PA
CBHW031443210526
45464CB00005B/2309